How to] without Having a "Job"

Get Paid From Home & Enjoy Your Life

Michael Greene

Table of Contents

Introduction

Chapter 1 - The Advantages of Working from Home

Chapter 2 – Things To Keep In Mind If Working At Home

Chapter 3 - Using the Internet to open the door to fresh opportunities

Chapter 4 - The Types of Jobs Available (Including 12 Jobs & 33 Websites)

Chapter 5 - Avoiding Scams on the Internet

Chapter 6 – Thirty Additional Freelance Websites To Get Started Today!

Conclusion

Highly Recommended Money Making Books

SPECIAL BONUS

Copyright 2014 by Globalized Healing, LLC - All rights reserved.

Introduction

I want to thank you for downloading the book, "How to Make Money without having a "Job": Enjoy Life & Get Paid from Home".

This book will help you discover additional income streams over the Internet more than just using it for entertainment—in the comfort of your own home.

You might have heard the news about America's down economy. But believe it or not, Uncle Sam's unemployment rate continues to grow in spite the disheartening news. Almost two million Americans quit their jobs every month. And the number one reason for leaving is that they don't like their boss.

If you consider finding another job or if you are just actively looking for one, there are plenty of opportunities waiting for you in the cyberspace. You can even enjoy life while getting paid from home. How? Is it possible? Don't worry, all the questions you have in mind are in this book, so just keep on reading and begin a new chapter in your life!

Chapter 1 - The Advantages of Working from Home

For all job-holders, "contentment" is one of the essential factors in sticking to a job. Sadly, many people are unsatisfied with their work and rarely exit the corporate world. They want relaxation, more time with family, and eventually more power for themselves, but are still afraid to take that leap and learn about the possibilities from working from home. If you are an employee, your time and decision-making will often depend on your boss's schedule.

Let's say your daughter has a school function and she's begging you to come. But then again, you also have to attend an important meeting at the office the same day. Which is more significant to you? Who are you going to choose—your boss waiting for your arrival or your daughter yearning for your presence?

It's quite challenging to shut one eye to your obligation as a parent and as a wage earner. You can make excuses and lose a job, or you can turn a deaf ear to your child's wishes and leave her heart broken. You do not have to choose if you are working from home; you are your own "boss", nobody will yell or throw a tantrum whatever your decision may be. Besides, working from home allows you to be flexible with your time. You have control over your schedule.

The facts are that more than 92% of American homes have an Internet connection. According to the U.S. Census Bureau, in 2008 more than $133.8 billion was made via the Internet. There is a lot of money to be had on the Internet on your laptop or home computer.

Nowadays, more and more people are quitting their day jobs. We can't find fault with them. They have their own reasons for leaving. If you're one of the crowds, you may find it hard to leave your "employee thinking" behind. But you can start anew this time—not as a wage earner but as an entrepreneur. You're now a freelancer, someone who sells your own business.

When you were an employee, you rely on your boss or your company when it comes to decision-making. This time, you don't only have to be decisive. You also have to be creative if you want to earn extra money. When you were an employee, you enjoy benefits and you really don't have to be pressured in paying for taxes. It will be automatically deducted from your monthly earnings. If you want to save a little money or pay for insurances even without a day job, it only takes a little discipline.

It allows you to do what you're passionate about. Being a freelancer, you can work on the things you love. This is what most freelancers like about their job. They enjoy working from home simply because it makes them happy—no pressures or hassles. In the first place, doing something you really don't like can be stressful and miserable. Now, you have the freedom to choose which projects you want to do. Besides, you won't be edgy to do things your own way. With the right tools, discipline, and a bit of hard work, you can be a lucrative writer, online marketer, virtual assistant, and the list goes on.

You'll never stop learning. Since you are in a business, you have to keep yourself updated with new trends, new things in your industry, as well as news around the world. Therefore, you will never stop learning. You'll eventually become enthusiastic to learn new knowledge from time to time. Best of all, you can apply those learnings in your personal life as well.

You'll discover limitless opportunities. There are tons of money-making opportunities waiting for you online. From content writing, copywriting, transcribing, up to web designing and the like, you have a number of careers to choose from.

It allows you to achieve a work-home balance. If you're a parent, you know how it feels to miss a single event in your child's life. But that's not going to happen if you manage your own time. You don't have to worry about cancelling business trips or important local meetings if your daughter has a school function.

Being in control of your own schedule also allows you to spend more time with your spouse and your friends.

You choose your rates. One perk of being a freelancer is you are free to set your own rates. So far, many freelancers are in doubt how much they should charge. It happens not just to newbies but also to long-time freelancers who would like to rearrange their charges with a client. To compute for your rates, you have to sum up your personal running costs, business operating rates, as well as taxes divided by the number of hours you worked.

You don't need a big amount of money to start up. If you already have a laptop and an Internet connection, you are all set to start working without ado. Unless you're an online seller and you just utilize the Internet to endorse your products, you don't need a huge amount of money to start up.

You won't be laid off by anyone. You are the "boss". Yes, you - job, you won't be fired or "laid-off". Just in case things didn't work with a previous client, you don't have to worry about losing a job for a week or two. There are plenty of fish in the sea. Clients are everywhere. Still, it will help to keep in mind that it's way easier to maintain a client than find a new one. You only have to communicate very well to avoid misunderstandings with a client. As a home-based worker, you don't have to depend on a corporation or on anyone else anymore when it comes to decision-making.

Chapter 2 – Things To Keep In Mind If Working At Home

Working in the comfort of your own home does not mean less work. Some people think that it's one of the advantages of home-based jobs. They eventually gave up their full-time careers to venture into something new, thinking that things will be at ease. In reality, freelancing also comes with obstacles. There will come a time when you'll get lazy to talk with clients or you'll lose confidence in your own skills. Or worse, you might regret leaving the corporate world—one with stable earnings, benefits, and company gatherings.

But if you're already there, in the middle of that jaunt they call freelancing, there's no room for regrets or laziness or losing confidence unless you don't have plans to succeed. The success of your home-based job lies on you. If you're planning to become a freelancer or already are, here are strategies you can do to enjoy life while getting paid:

Manage your time accordingly. As a freelancer, you have the freedom to accept tons of workloads. You may not have a boss to remind you about work being late. But there are clients waiting for you to update or submit your work. Overlooking deadlines can only mean one thing—losing a client. And losing one also means losing money and opportunity. It's way easier to keep a client than try to search for a new one.

Organize your workplace. While home is the most comfortable place to work at, you can't help but find yourself sleepy or lazy at times. To become extra productive, it helps to work in a place where you won't be tempted to sleep or lie down. As much as possible, do not work in your bedroom. But if you really don't have a choice, you can set up a mini office in your own room. Most importantly, organize your space so that you can become more productive to work.

Set your boundaries. Online gigs can be addictive. Genuinely speaking, it will demand some of your time, effort, and money. You might be too passionate with your online business that you forget other things in life. Next thing you know, you'll find yourself exhausted the way you do when you're still a regular wage earner. So set up your boundaries before your home-based gig consumes all of your time, resources, and energy.

Ask around to confirm the credibility of the sites you visit. As with anything on the Internet, you have to be extra careful especially now that illegitimate and bogus sites are on the rampage. Some websites offer rates that seem too good to be true. To avoid online swindlers, research first about your employer's websites and check them out before signing up for a job.

You should price accordingly. Establish a reasonable hourly or fixed rate. One of the biggest blunders a freelancer makes is come up with a very cheap rate. If you're new to home-based business, it's logical that you set up affordable rates for your clients. But if that's too cheap that it does not match your workload, it won't hurt to increase your rate. After all, your rate also signifies your service value. On the contrary, it will be a challenge to attract clients if your rates are too high especially if you are a newbie. Therefore, it's important to look at standard rates for the service your providing and adjust it for what you need.

Use a time-tracking app so you won't forget about deadlines. This time, nobody else will remind you to submit your work. You have to be meticulous in following deadlines especially now that some of your projects are urgently needed for submission. But as human nature, you might forget that you only have a few hours remaining for a certain assignment. Thus, you can download a time-tracking app that reminds you of your commitment as a freelancer.

Remove distractions. Unless you are an online seller who uses Twitter or Facebook to promote your business you may have to bump off unnecessary stuff (time wasting sites, Facebook, email, etc.) in the workplace to increase productivity.

Inevitably, one of the most intriguing questions you'll have in mind is "Can I earn decent money working from home?" The answer is yes, it is conceivable for anyone to get passive income with home-based jobs. Depending on your income needs, you can choose to work full-time and earn sufficiently.

Anyone would like to know how much he or she could earn with freelancing. If you are just starting out, you surely want to know how you can earn money quickly. Needless to say, freelancing isn't a get-rich-quick job but it makes sense to say that many people earned serious money working in the comforts of their own homes. You too can join the flock of thriving home-based workers.

As a freelancer, getting at the top of the tree is a conspiracy of skills, motivation, and hard work. The first thing you have to do is know what you're really good at. From there, you can start selling your stuff or your services online. Again, how much you'll get will only depend on you. More labor only means more money.

Christine, a work-at-home mom, started a travel agency right from her home office in 2006. She's now working as a travel agent while enjoying more time with her kids. As a home-based travel agent, another perk of her job is that she gets great discounts when she decided to take her family on a vacation.

But the story does not end here. As much as we'd like to think that home-based job is a dream job, we have to think again and come back to reality. As an entrepreneur, you'll still be paying taxes. More than half of employed Americans own a small business and many of them have home offices. Apparently, they also pay contributions.

The Skills Needed

Communication skills

Effective communication is a necessary in any kind of job. If you are planning to work as an online English tutor, call center representative, or transcriptionist, you have to be proficient in understanding several accents and slangs. Plus, you'll be negotiating with your clients from time to time so you have to communicate very well in order to avoid false interpretations.

Creativity

One of the good things about home business is that it allows you to use your creativity. If you want to get more out of your home-based career, you have to exert more creativity especially in promoting your products or services. If you are a freelance writer, you may set up a blog about freelance writing and have your friends know about it. If you're an online marketer, you may sign up on various social media websites to inform others about your business.

Office skills

If you're planning to become a virtual assistant, you have to handle administrative tasks. But this time, you don't have to pressure yourself in getting the hang of several accents or dialects. You won't be required to answer or make phone calls. You simply have to do things via e-mail.

Editing skills

Proofreading and editing skills are a must for copywriters. If you want to venture into copywriting and focus on direct marketing or advertising, it's time to work on your grammar and language expertise.

Aside from copywriting, content writing and transcribing jobs also entail high attention to detail.

Chapter 3 - Using the Internet to open the door to fresh opportunities

The Internet is not only there for our entertainment. The good news is that we can now use it as a source of income. And it won't really take a lot of stake—just have a computer with a high-speed connection and you're all set. During these trying times, you have to be more creative in finding many ways to earn. By a happy chance, you can have the Internet as your gateway to new opportunities.

Here's how you can maximize its use and eventually get additional income:

It allows you to promote yourself. With free blogging platforms such as WordPress and Blogger, you can put up your online portfolio to publicize your products and services. You can do it yourself or hire someone create it for you. You just have to make sure that you own a professional URL for employers to browse. It will also help to have your online résumé brief and updated. Once you start getting regular or large amounts of visitors to your blog (which can take sometimes 6-months to a year, depending on how much marketing you do) you can begin making money with Google Adsense, where you post a code to your blog or website and Ads will appear.

If you want to watch an amazing short 5 minute video on how people have been making $100's extra each month with Google, be sure to click here. Every time someone clicks on that ad and buys the product, you'll get a commission.

You can earn more without investing much. Internet home-based businesses are easy to set up. You don't need an angel investor to cash in on your first step.

There is a site called Kickstarter where people post ideas that they are passionate about and try to raise money for the project. A few of the categories include Film, Dance, Fashion, and Food. The most successful projects usually have videos talking about the cause or how passionate they are about the project.

You don't need a formal education to launch your business. You can even start even without a computer. With smartphones featuring email services and fast browsers, you can get started with the least amount of expense and make money even if you're not at home.

It allows you to resell your stuff online. You don't have to throw stuff out that works. You can sell it at a cheap price over the Internet. You can also start a buy and sell business online, using E-bay or Amazon.

Chapter 4 - The Types of Jobs Available (Including 12 Jobs & 33 Websites)

Now we get to the juicy stuff – the actual things you can do for a career at home. This section will cover jobs that you can work both part-time and full-time, depending on your life schedule.

Content Writer

These days, many companies need writers to market their products and services. There are a number targeted websites for particular niches you can actually write about—travel, health, beauty, and so on. All you have to do is write articles on a range of topics. Afterwards, you'll be asked to submit your written work via e-mail or online portal. There are many sites that freelance writers use nowadays including:

- Absolute Write - a ton of quality content and thousands of international listings

- FWO Intl - free site with thousands of listings

- Media Bistro - an upcoming site that more and more people are going to each day

- Pro Blogger – for people who love to blog, and want to make an income out of it

If you love writing and enjoy all-types of writing, including article-writing, stories, movie scripts, and blogs be sure to check this out to earn good money.

Affiliate Marketing

In this you are essentially the middleman. In this business you set it up, for example a website platform, and the business runs itself. The affiliate receives a commission for referring customer from their website platform to the merchant- usually a percentage of the sale.

Amazon Affiliates for example are common and have been highly successful. The affiliates would establish their own website and use a code generated by Amazon to sell Amazon's products. When a sale was made, both the affiliate and Amazon would make a percentage of the sale.

For an affiliate marketing website to be successful, it needs to have high traffic, The more traffic and more clicks and affiliate can generate, the higher the earnings. One of the advantages is that once you have a successful affiliate site up, it almost becomes a passive income and you will be able to put it on autopilot while you create and launch another affiliate website.

You are able to both sell products you've created, as well as sell products that are created by other companies.

A few of the best sites (besides Amazon Affiliates – as mentioned above) to check out for products include:

1. Clickbank - which is the most popular database for online affiliate products

2. JV Notify - which gives a list of hot and upcoming products in the affiliate market.

3. Warrior Forum - which is a huge Internet Marketing Forum, and an excellent way to get connected with other entrepreneurs

4. JV Network- which has thousands of products according to their niches, and is a great resource for finding product launches

Here are a few books for beginners to Affiliate Marketing that I recommend:

One is by Patrick Kennedy titled, How To Make A Ton of Money With Affiliate Marketing, which covers the details about how to get started with affiliate marketing so that you can be on your way to making a passive income.

The other one I wrote in 2013. It's titled, Make Money With Clickbank, where I cover the details about getting started with Clickbank – which again, is the largest affiliate marketing database. It gets you off to a quick start, skipping over several of the months of trial and error that I went through when first starting out a few years ago.

If you're interested in getting started affiliate marketing, I highly recommend you watch this video. It was designed by Patric Chan, who has become a top-seller on Clickbank Affiliate Marketing. Click Here To View It.

 Also, beware of the get-rich-quick schemes. Much of starting out in affiliate marketing will be trial and error and simply finding out what works and what doesn't.

Online Tutor

With the foray of Asians wanting to learn English in order to become more competitive in the global job market, this gig is very in-demand right now. Also, math and science are fields that are challenging for many, so tutoring jobs in these fields are common too. There are websites that people seek out to find tutors for these areas – which you can place yourself on if you'd like to tutor.

Many people have launched businesses via Skype in order to learn English with people from other countries. Of course it also involves advertising and getting your business out there, which can be done through many social media websites including:

www.facebook.com, www.linkedin.com, and your own website.

One side-note I wanted to mention, is that there is a way to make money online using Facebook – why not make money if you are on FB anyway, right? Anyway click here to watch a short video on how to make money using Facebook.

However, your working hours will depend on your student's time zone. That can either become an advantage or disadvantage for you depending on your set-up. You can choose to take it on a part-time or a full-time basis.

A few of the best sites for freelancers include:

- Class Do
- Freelancer

Fiverr

One of the newest websites launched in 2011 is fiverr.com. This is an excellent source that allows people to use their own talents to make money. This could include proofreading a document of 1000 words, doing SEO for a website, or singing happy birthday to a video camera. The options seem endless.

All projects start at $5, and can take as little as a few minutes, and other projects can take a few hours and you can earn anywhere between $5 and $60. All

"Gigs" start at $5 the first month, and if you have a good customer status and feedback you will be promoted to making more money.

To check it out go to:

- Fiverr

*If you want to get off to a fast start and make money with Fiverr, I recommend a book by Patrick Kennedy titled, Ways To Make Money Using Fiverr. It shows you how to get setup fast, and recommends 25 of the top "gigs" for 2014 so you can get off to a solid start.

Logo Designer

There are many online businesses these days and every day there is practically thousands of new ones popping up. At the same time freelancing for designing logos at a competitive price has become in great demand. There are several sites online you can join now and submit your work online that allow people to look at your work. From there, if a customer likes your work they can select you to design their logo.

Some of these sites include:

- O-Desk - which is a platform for developers working from home.
- 99 Designs

Website Developers

The demand for websites is increasing. Although there are many easy-to-build websites databases such as www.weebly.com, there are many people who want help designing and setting up their website. Wordpress is still one of the largest used to build a website and let's face it, people don't want to take the time to figure out Wordpress if they don't have to. This is where a Wordpress Expert could go in and build the website at the buyers request.

If you have skill and like to develop websites from scratch then that is a great avenue to venture. Again, websites are still in demand and more people everyday are trying to work from home and escape the corporate world in order to spend more time with their family and live the life they want to live.

Again, O-Desk is an excellent platform to get on if you are talented or have experience developing websites and/or using Wordpress.

- Get A Freelancer - a ton of listings although this site warns you to be cautious for fraudsters

- Microlancer - just merged microlance and freelance, and has become one of the biggest for database platforms for freelancers

SEO Specialist

A Search Engine Optimization Specialist is important in today's world. They help websites to rank high on Internet Search Engines such as Google and Yahoo. The higher the ranking, the more potential business the company will have. Therefore, an SEO Specialist helps to make this happen.

Sites you can list yourself include:

- <u>Scriptlance</u> - thousands use this site everyday
- <u>Freelancer - Get Hired</u>

Mobile App Developer

If you want to begin developing and/or learning how to make apps for phones, this is a booming industry right now. It is becoming just as popular, if not more than websites. The only "challenge" is that coding languages and technical skills are required, so it is not easy if you are brand new to it. There are many books nowadays to learn the coding languages as well as schools that teach the languages, so you can learn it effectively.

Some noteworthy sites to list yourself on include:

- Project 4 Hire
- Get A Coder

Personal Assistant

Personal Assistants are becoming in higher and higher demand, especially with more entrepreneurs. They are similar to an entrepreneur's right hand man (or woman) and they often do the office management tasks. These include answering phone calls via their P.A's cell phone or home phone, scheduling meetings and reminding the Entrepreneur of the meeting, coordinating travel plans. Generally it is key to have excellent organization skills and top communication skills with this field. The more experience you have, the more you can charge, and people will gladly pay it too.

Some of the sites you can list yourself on include:

- E-Lance - online portal to network with many business professionals
- O-Desk

*If you know how to use YouTube, upload videos, and post comments, and want to earn money doing it, you should check out this video because it is one of the easiest and legitimate ways I've found to make money online using a product called TubeLaunch. Click here to watch the video (which is a little cheesy, but the product is great).

Translator/Transcriber

Simply listen to audio files and write them down. Transcribing isn't really a very mental-challenging task but you need to be adept in proofreading and understanding accents, and be skilled and speedy using a keyboard. It's also an advantage if you master of idioms, figures of speech, and spelling. The potential income depends on the audio length or description as well as the urgency of the project.

Take a look at these websites:

- SDL - one of the most recognized companies for freelance writers
- Mturk
- E-Lance
- O-Desk

If you're ready to get started now with translating simple documents, articles and videos, click here because here is how you can start getting paid (spots are limited).

Life Coach

This is a fairly new career, and it is rapidly growing. The reason I am listing this here is because it is primarily done over the phone and Skype, so generally it is done at home.

It can be highly rewarding because of the amount of impact you can have on people's lives. It involves working with people 1-on-1 to help them discover their life purpose, finding out what they really want in life; setting goals and motivating them to achieve them- whether it be with health (e.g. losing weight), relationship (helping them learn what they want in relationships), or career (discover a career that suits their personality and that is fulfilling for them). That is just covering the surface of what a life coach can do.

*To learn more, take a look at this book by Daniel Robbins titled, [How To Be A Powerful Life Coach](). It's a quick read to open your eyes to what is possible as a life coach. It also gives great insight on how to get more clients as a life coach, and earn a good living.

If you want to learn more about life coaching, I recommend the book by Henry Kimsy-House, titled [Co-Active Coaching](). It goes into detail about life coaching and how to be one. It was written by the Founder of The Coaches Training Institute, which is a well-known and widely recognized life-coaching school.

Trading Online

Binary Options, and Stocks are challenging and can be very risky (especially binary options), but it can be very financially rewarding as well. It is in a sense gambling, especially if you aren't given the best tools to get started, and successful strategies to continue. Also, it is very important to do your research and determine which sites are best for you and your finances. In addition, there are scams out there, so again do thorough research before investing any money. It is good to take a look at legitimate customer reviews.

Here are a few sites to get you started:

- Traderush
- Redwood
- Optionfair
- Scottrade

*I wanted to share a video with you that got was one of the methods I used when first getting started with Forex/Currency trading (and winning). Click here to watch it.

For more information, I've written a Binary Options books for beginners, and one on Investments listed here:

- Forex Trading
- Binary Options
- Investments

Online Surveys

This has been an upcoming and effective way to earn money online. It really does not take much effort and has proven over and over again to allow individuals to work from home, and only put in a few hours of work each week. Below are two links to show you how to get started.

Chapter 5 - Avoiding Scams on the Internet

While you enjoy searching for new gigs online, fraudsters are also taking the moment to hunt for their next victims. In the second chapter, we learned that it's a must to be extra cautious in visiting various websites. Now that the Internet is also a place for trade and selling, there are people out there who take advantage of online marketers. To avoid scams over the Internet, here are things you should do and shouldn't do as a freelancer or a home-based business owner:

Never pay for sites that promise to give back something big in return. There are websites that assure high-paying jobs while working at home. The drawback is that you have to pay them for start-up. Be careful about these sites that ask you to pay something before landing a job. There are great chances that these sites are purely bogus.

Stay away in investing over the Internet. There's no sure thing in investing through the Internet. Don't trust people who ask you to invest in something you are not sure of.

Do a research of company names and websites. Before you register for an online gig, it's best to know first if your future employer is someone to trust. There are freelancers who lose confidence in pursuing their home-based careers thinking that others will only fool them. While there are opportunists over the Internet, there are also nice and trustworthy people who respect their fellow online workers.

Don't send money to people you don't know. Needless to say, you don't trust a stranger who asks money from the Internet. Avoid people who insist you to send cash using wire transfers.

Don't give personal information to anyone. One of the greatest things we're taught as kids is not to talk to strangers. If someone you don't know ask for your information, never ever give it because they might use these things to scam you.

Report scams. If you're already tricked online, don't ignore it. If you're an online seller and you were victimized by scammers, you can file a complaint at the Federal Trade Commission. When things get worse, you can even report it with the attorney general of your state.

Chapter 6 – Thirty Additional Freelance Websites To Get Started Today!

Content Writing

- www.writeraccess.com
- www.problogger.com
- http://www.freelancewriting.com/freelance-writing-jobs.php
- http://www.textbroker.com/
- http://www.wordgigs.com/

Affiliate Marketing

- http://www.freelancer.com/jobs/affiliate-marketing

Online Tutor

- http://www.berlitz.com/Careers/33/

- http://classof1.com/careers
- http://www.homeworkhelp.com/tutorjoinus.php
- http://www.aim4a.com/tutors.php
- http://www.eduwizards.com/index.php
- http://www.tutor.com/apply
- http://www.alphatutors.co.uk/careers/Freelance-Teacher/

Logo Designers

- http://www.guru.com

Website Developers

- http://www.freelancer.com/#rac
- http://www.getacoder.com/
- http://jobs.smashingmagazine.com/

SEO Specialist

- www.ifreelance.com/freelance-jobs/seo-freelance-jobs
- www.freelancer.com/jobs/SEO/
- www.craigslist.com

Mobile App Developers

- https://www.odesk.com/o/profiles/.../mobile-application-development/
- www.peopleperhour.com/freelance/application+developer
- www.freelancer.com/work/freelance-mobile-app-developer

Personal Assistant

- www.peopleperhour.com/freelance/personal+assistant
- http://www.ifreelance.com/freelance-jobs/personal-assistant-freelance-jobs/
- http://www.savvysugar.com/Freelance-Personal-Assistants-23164735
-

Translator/Transcriber

- http://www.proz.com/
- http://www.translatorscafe.com/cafe/JobPost.asp
- http://www.rev.com/freelancers/transcription
- http://www.freelancer.com/jobs/Transcription/

Conclusion

I hope this book was able to help you see the wide array of opportunities there are from working from home. I also hope that you have an idea of what path you can take or might want to take to begin working from home, being your own boss, and living the life you want to live.

Thank you and I wish you the best!

Made in the USA
Middletown, DE
10 November 2015